A place to spill your guts.

This book is formatted so you can express yourself any way you wish. Write. Draw. Collage. Dialogue. Pie chart. Finger paint. Do what ever you feel. Just get it out.

- The Angry Therapist

What you said.

INT. _____ -

YOU

THEM

YOU

THEM

YOU

What you should have said.

INT. _____ -

                    YOU

                    THEM

                    YOU

                    THEM

                    YOU

PSEUDO SELF

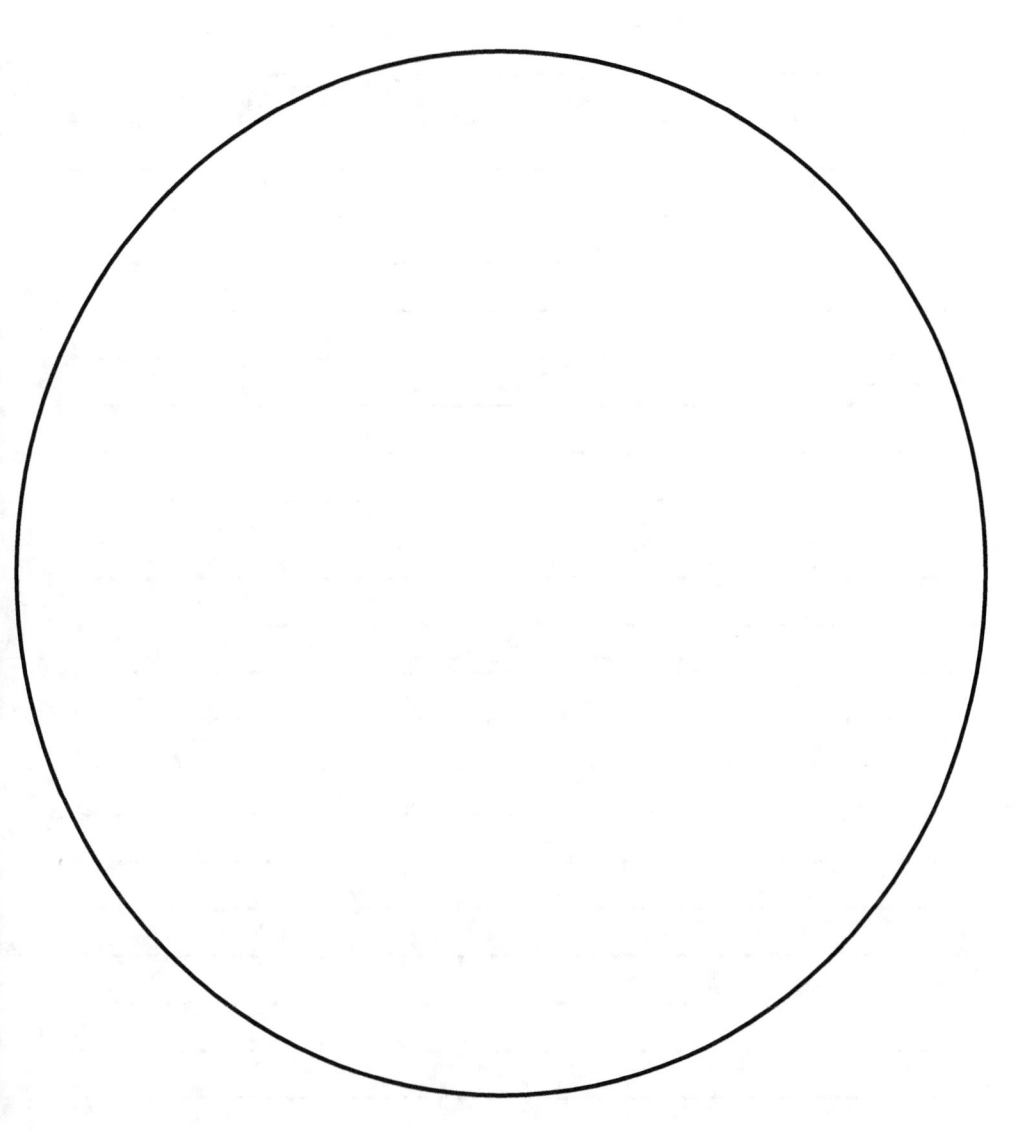

What you said.

INT. _____ -

                        YOU

                        THEM

                        YOU

                        THEM

                        YOU

What you should have said.

INT. _____ -

YOU

THEM

YOU

THEM

YOU

Splash.

Splash.

Splash.

Splash.

Splash.

Splash.

PSEUDO SELF

PSEUDO SELF

Splash.

What you said.

INT. _____ -

YOU

THEM

YOU

THEM

YOU

What you should have said.

INT. _____ -

                    YOU

                    THEM

                    YOU

                    THEM

                    YOU

Genogram.

A pictorial display of a person's family relationships.

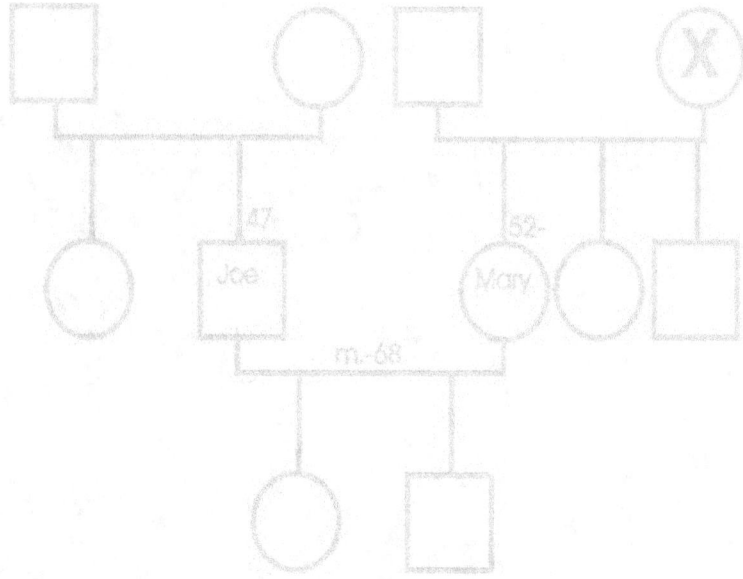

Now draw yours.

Try to do three generations.

Circle = Female
Square = Male

Draw a squiggly line = tension
A = Addict or Asshole
Double parallel line = Who you're close to
X = Emotionally cut off from family

Feelings / thoughts about your Genogram.

_____

_____

_____

_____

_____

_____

_____

_____

_____

_____

_____

_____

_____

_____

_____

_____

_____

_____

_____

_____

_____

_____

_____

What you said.

INT. _____ -

YOU

THEM

YOU

THEM

YOU

What you should have said.

INT. _____ -

                              YOU

                              THEM

                              YOU

                              THEM

                              YOU

Splash.

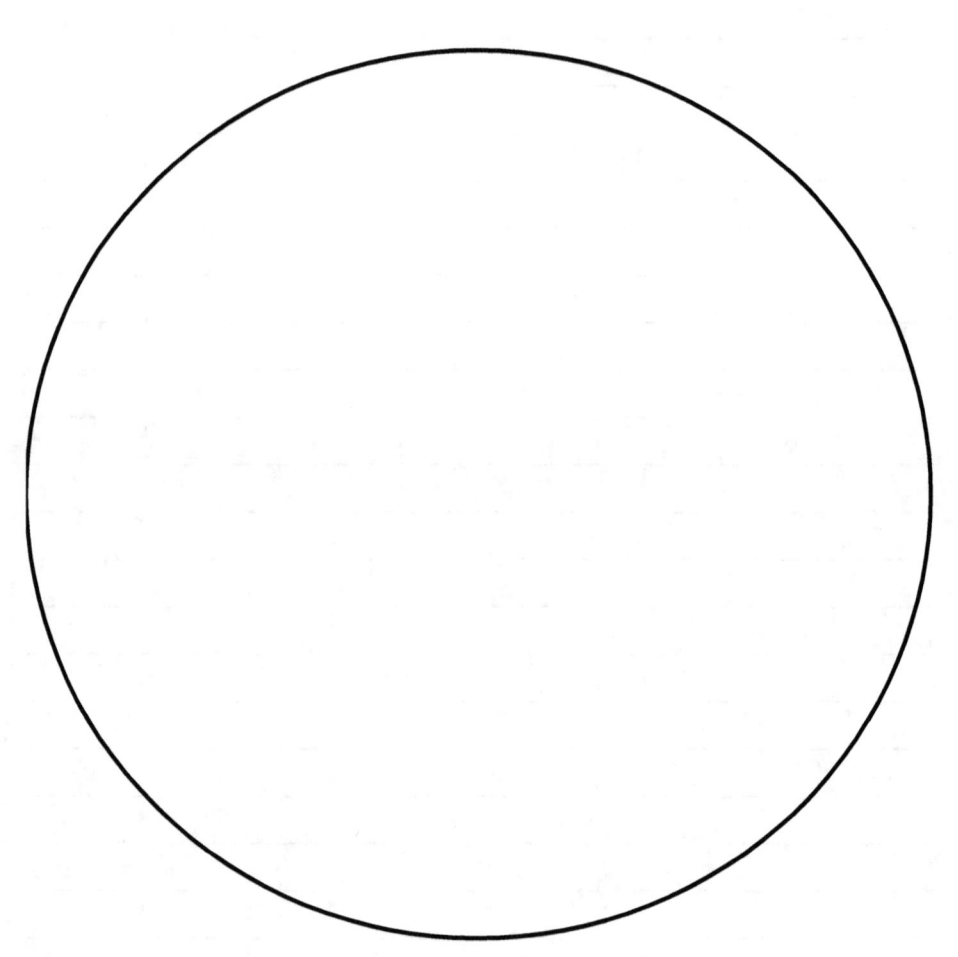

Splash.

Splash.

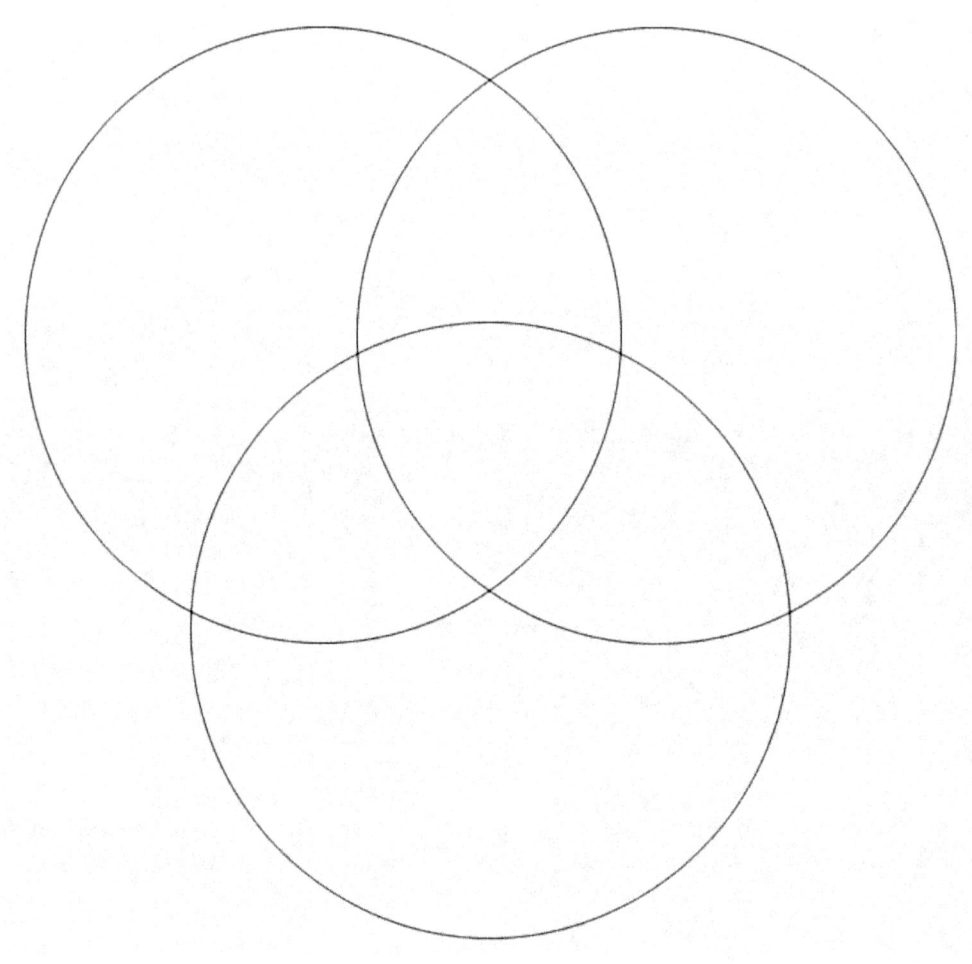

Splash.

Splash.

Splash.

What you said.

INT. _____ -

                                    YOU

                                    THEM

                                    YOU

                                    THEM

                                    YOU

What you should have said.

INT. _____ -

YOU

THEM

YOU

THEM

YOU

PSEUDO SELF

Splash.

Splash.

Splash.

Splash.

Splash.

Your Life as a Movie Trailer.

Describe your life as if you just saw it as a movie trailer. Genre, music, dialogue, etc.

_____

_____

_____

_____

_____

_____

_____

_____

_____

_____

_____

_____

_____

_____

_____

_____

_____

_____

_____

_____

Splash.

What you said.

INT. _____ -

YOU

THEM

YOU

THEM

YOU

What you should have said.

INT. _____ -

                    YOU

                    THEM

                    YOU

                    THEM

                    YOU

Splash.

Destination Postcard.

Describe where you see yourself in five years. What are you doing? Where are you living? Who are you with? How have you changed? Emotionally, physically, spiritually? Who are you?

_____

_____

_____

_____

_____

_____

_____

_____

_____

_____

_____

_____

_____

_____

_____

_____

_____

_____

_____

www.theangrytherapist.com

www.ingramcontent.com/pod-product-compliance
Lightning Source LLC
Chambersburg PA
CBHW071355310526
45789CB00020B/296